NOTE TO PARENTS

Welcome to Kingfisher Readers! This program is designed to help young readers build skills, confidence, and a love of reading as they explore their favorite topics.

These tips can help you get more from the experience of reading books together. But remember, the most important thing is to make reading fun!

Tips to Warm Up Before Reading

- Look through the book with your child. Ask them what they notice about the pictures.
- Wonder aloud together. Ask questions and make predictions. What will this book be about? What are some words we could expect to find on these pages?

While Reading

- Take turns or read together until your child takes over.
- Point to the words as you say them.
- When your child gets stuck on a word, ask if the picture could help. Then think about the first letter too.
- Accept and praise your child's contributions.

After Reading

- Look back at the things your child found interesting. Encourage connections to other things you both know.
- Draw pictures or make models to explore these ideas.
- Read the book again soon, to build fluency.

With five distinct levels and a wealth of appealing topics, the Kingfisher Readers series provides children with an exciting way to learn to read about the world around them. Enjoy!

Ellie Costa, M.S. Ed.
Literacy Specialist, Bank Street School for Children, New York

KINGFISHER READERS

level 2

What We Eat

Brenda Stones

KINGFISHER

NEW YORK

KINGFISHER
LONDON & NEW YORK

Copyright © Kingfisher 2014
Published in the United States by Kingfisher,
175 Fifth Ave., New York, NY 10010
Kingfisher is an imprint of Macmillan Children's Books, London.
All rights reserved.

Distributed in the U.S. and Canada by Macmillan,
175 Fifth Ave., New York, NY 10010

Library of Congress Cataloging-in-Publication data
has been applied for.

Series editor: Thea Feldman
Literacy consultant: Ellie Costa, Bank Street School for Children, New York

ISBN: 978-0-7534-7120-3 (HB)
ISBN: 978-0-7534-7121-0 (PB)

Kingfisher books are available for special promotions
and premiums. For details contact: Special Markets
Department, Macmillan, 175 Fifth Ave., New York, NY 10010.

For more information, please visit
www.kingfisherbooks.com

Printed in China
9 8 7 6 5 4 3 2 1
1TR/0314/WKT/UG/105MA

Contents

We need food to live!

Food helps us grow and stay **healthy**.

It gives us **energy** to run and play.

Food tastes good too
and is fun to share with friends!

Time to eat!

Many people have breakfast in the morning.

They have lunch in the middle of the day.

Then they eat dinner in the evening.

What is your favorite meal of the day?

On your plate

You need to eat the right foods
to stay healthy and strong.

Here are different kinds of foods.

Look how often you should eat them!

Eat some **lean** meat, fish, eggs, nuts, or beans every day.

Eat some milk, cheese, or yogurt every day.

Eat some bread, rice, or pasta every day.

Eat cake, chocolate, or fried foods only once in a while.

Eat a lot of fruits and vegetables every day.

Fruits and vegetables

Half of what you eat each day should be fruits and vegetables.

Fruits and vegetables have a lot of **nutrients** in them that are good for your body.

Fruits and vegetables grow on plants all over the world.

All fruits have **seeds** in them.

Bread, rice, and pasta

Bread, rice, and pasta are all made from **grains**.

Wheat and rye are two kinds of grains.

Half of the grains
you eat every day
should be **whole grains**.

Meat, fish, eggs, and beans

Meat, fish, and eggs
are all **proteins**.

Proteins help your bones and muscles grow.

Beans, nuts, and lentils are proteins too.

They are good proteins for people who are **vegetarians**.

Milk, cheese, and yogurt

Milk, cheese, and yogurt
are all **dairy** foods.

Dairy foods help build your bones.

Milk can come from cows, goats, or sheep.

Milk can be made into cheese, yogurt, or ice cream!

Drink up!

What should you drink?

Milk and water are good drinks for growing children.

Your body needs a lot of water.

Every day you should drink about six glasses of water.

Juice can be a good drink too,
but it has a lot of sugar in it,
so a small glass is best.

Food from the farm

A lot of our food comes from farms.

Farmers grow grains,
fruits, and vegetables.

They raise animals for milk
and meat.

Cutting a field
of grain on
a farm

Food travels
by boat or plane
so one day it can
get to you!

Making food ready to eat

Some food goes from the farm to a **factory**, where it is made ready to eat.

For instance, grains are made into flour and then bread.

The bread is packed and shipped to the store.

Food shopping

You can buy food from a small store, a big supermarket, or an outdoor market.

Some stores sell just one kind of food, like fish.

Other stores sell hundreds of different foods!

Cooking a meal

There are many different ways
to cook food.

A pot placed on the stove
can be used to boil some foods.

A wok
cooks foods
quickly.

An oven is used to bake foods
like this hot, crispy pizza.

Foods of the world

The foods your family eats may come from places near or far.

Rice grows in many places, including China and India.

Yams, which are like potatoes, grow in many African countries.

What foods grow where you live?

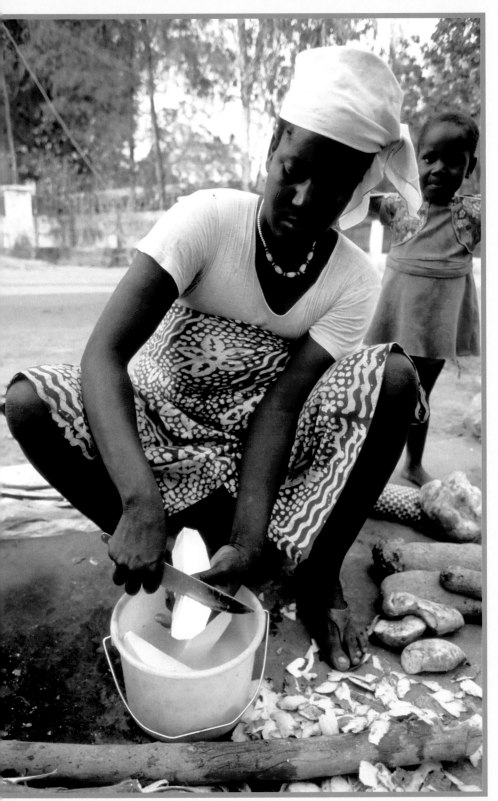

Festive foods

Every special day has its special foods.

Many people have cake on their birthday!

For Thanksgiving, many people eat turkey.

For **Diwali**, many people eat sweet foods.

What is your favorite holiday? What do you eat then?

Glossary

dairy milk, and foods made from milk

Diwali the Hindu "Festival of Lights"

energy the power that drives our bodies

factory a place where things are made

grains a major food group that includes wheat

healthy fit and well

lean having little or no fat

nutrients the healthy things in foods

proteins foods, such as meat, that help your bones and muscles grow

seeds hard pieces inside fruits from which new plants grow

vegetarian someone who does not eat animals

whole grains grains that are left whole or natural

If you have enjoyed reading
this book, look out for more in
the Kingfisher Readers series!

Collect
and read
them all!

KINGFISHER READERS: LEVEL 2

Amazing Animal Senses ☐
Fur and Feathers ☐
In the Rainforest ☐
Sun, Moon, and Stars ☐
Trucks ☐
What Animals Eat ☐
What We Eat ☐
Where Animals Live ☐
Where We Live ☐
Your Body ☐

KINGFISHER READERS: LEVEL 3

Ancient Rome ☐
Cars ☐
Creepy Crawlies ☐
Dinosaur World ☐
Firefighters ☐
Record Breakers—The Biggest ☐
Vikings ☐
Volcanoes ☐

For a full list of Kingfisher Readers books, plus
guidance for teachers and parents and activities
and fun stuff for kids, go to the Kingfisher Readers
website: **www.kingfisherreaders.com**